Belongs to:

____

____

www.ingramcontent.com/pod-product-compliance
Lightning Source LLC
Chambersburg PA
CBHW052036280526
45791CB00010B/2980
9781073637423